THE Relaxation COLORING BOOK

THE
Relaxation
COLORING BOOK

Gorgeous images to calm and inspire

Patience Coster

SIRIUS

SIRIUS

This edition published in 2022 by Sirius Publishing, a division of
Arcturus Publishing Limited,
26/27 Bickels Yard, 151–153 Bermondsey Street,
London SE1 3HA

ISBN: 978-1-3988-1864-4
CH004839NT

Printed in India by Multivista Global Pvt.Ltd

Introduction

Shading a picture in colors of your choice generates a sense of stillness and wellness. It stimulates brain areas related to motor skills and creativity and works as a relaxation technique, calming the mind and occupying the hands.

The Relaxation Coloring Book contains gorgeous images of birds, leaves, flowers, fish, butterflies, and tranquil landscapes to soothe the mind and please the senses. By coloring in the outlines you will de-stress your mind and body and create your own beautiful artwork. So put your worries on hold, pick up your crayons, pencils or felt-tips, and get in touch with your creative side.

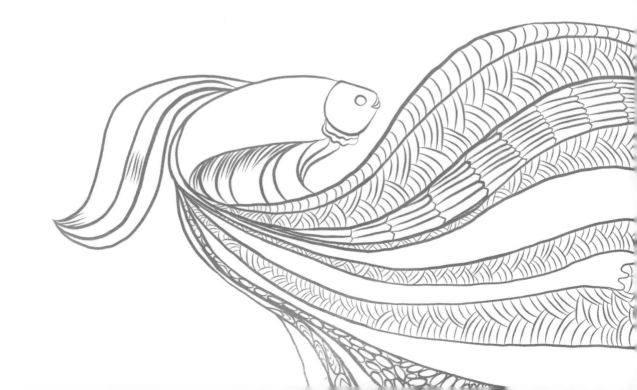

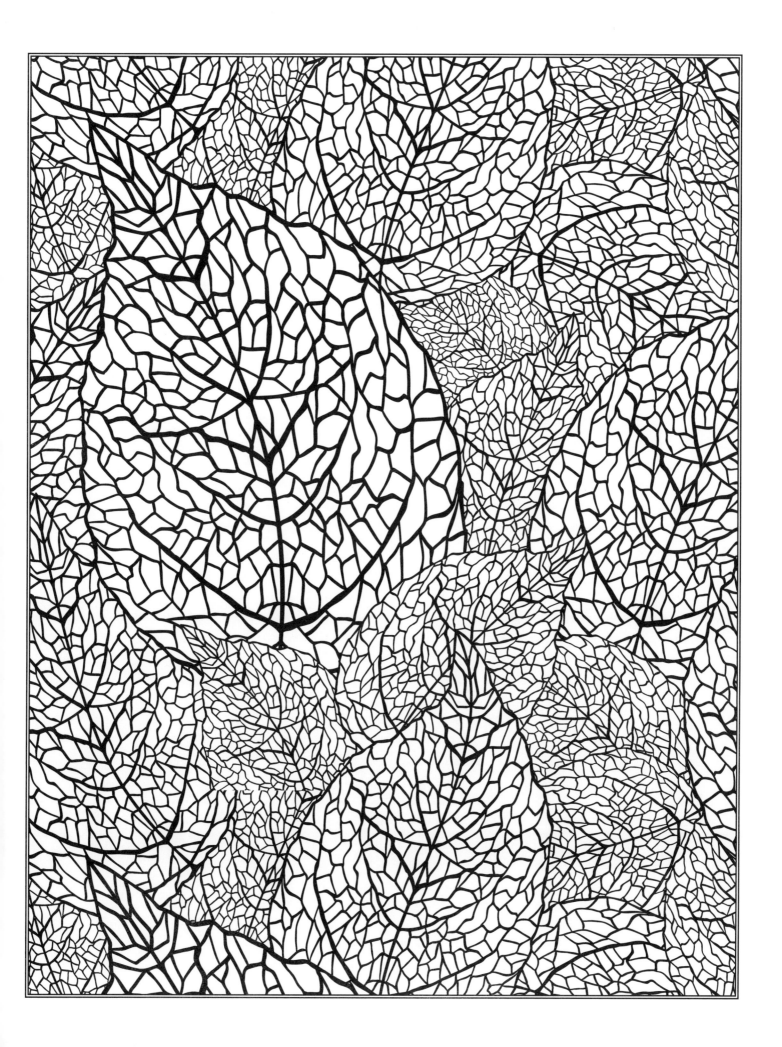